W9-AAE-071

TROPICAL RAINFORESTS

SEYMOUR SIMON

 Smithsonian  Collins

An Imprint of HarperCollins*Publishers*

Special thanks to Beth King, Science Interpreter, Smithsonian Tropical
Research Institute, for her invaluable contribution to this book.

PHOTO CREDITS: page 2: © Jacques Jangoux/Photo Researchers, Inc.; page 3: © John Kaprvielian/Photo Researchers, Inc.; pages 4–5: © Nature's Images/Photo Researchers, Inc.; page 6 (from left to right): © Art Wolfe/Photo Researchers, Inc.; © Fletcher & Baylis/Photo Researchers, Inc.; © Steve Cooper/Photo Researchers, Inc.; page 7: © Art Wolfe/Photo Researchers, Inc.; page 8: © Gregory G. Dimijian, M.D./Photo Researchers, Inc.; page 10: © Jacques Jangoux/Photo Researchers, Inc.; page 11: © Art Wolfe/ Photo Researchers, Inc.; pages 12–13: © Dr. George Beccaloni/Photo Researchers, Inc.; pages 14–15: © Tierbild Okapia/Photo Researchers, Inc.; page 16: © Adam Jones/Photo Researchers, Inc.; page 17 (from left to right): © Craig K. Lorenz/Photo Researchers, Inc.; © Stephen Dalton/Photo Researchers, Inc.; © David M. Schleser/Nature's Images/Photo Researchers, Inc.; page 18: © Art Wolfe/Photo Researchers, Inc.; page 19: © Stephen Dalton/Photo Researchers, Inc.; page 20: © Chris Gallagher/ Photo Researchers, Inc.; page 21 (from left to right): © Tom McHugh/Photo Researchers, Inc.; © George Steinmetz/Corbis; page 23: © Tom McHugh/Photo Researchers, Inc.; page 24: © Tom Brakefield/Corbis; page 26: © Ken Thomas/Photo Researchers, Inc.; page 27: © Tom McHugh/Photo Researchers, Inc.; pages 28–29: © Mark Bowler/Photo Researchers, Inc.; page 30: © Fletcher & Baylis/Photo Researchers, Inc.; pages 30–31: © Will & Deni McIntyre/Photo Researchers, Inc.

Library of Congress Cataloging-in-Publication Data
Simon, Seymour.
    Tropical rainforests / Seymour Simon. — 1st ed.
        p.   cm.
    ISBN 978-0-06-114253-6 (trade bdg.) — ISBN 978-0-06-114254-3 (lib. bdg.)
    1. Rain forests—Juvenile literature.   I. Title.
QH86.S555   2010   2009031420
578.734—dc22   CIP
                                                                                                   AC

10 11 12 13 14   SCP   10 9 8 7 6 5 4 3 2 1
❖
First Edition

To Liz
with my love

Smithsonian Mission Statement

For more than 160 years, the Smithsonian has remained true to its mission, "the increase and diffusion of knowledge." Today the Smithsonian is not only the world's largest provider of museum experiences supported by authoritative scholarship in science, history, and the arts but also an international leader in scientific research and exploration. The Smithsonian offers the world a picture of America, and America a picture of the world.

Imagine being surrounded by thick walls of green plants. All around you are roots, vines, bushes, and trees. Even though the sun is high in the sky, you're in dense shade and it feels like twilight. Water drips steadily from leaves and collects in puddles on the damp ground. The humid air feels heavy against your skin. Choruses of insect, frog, and bird calls fill the air. You hear dozens of other sounds too, strange ones that you can't identify. You are in a tropical rainforest.

Tropical rainforests are warm, wet places found near the equator. Almost every day, you might find yourself in a downpour of huge rain droplets. A rainforest gets at least 60 inches of rain a year and the average temperature is above 77° Fahrenheit. This is like being in Miami and southern Florida during the summer. But in tropical rainforests, one season is much like the next. Most plants keep their leaves and grow all year long.

The largest rainforests are found in Central America, South America, central Africa, and Southeast Asia. There are also smaller rainforests on rainy islands, coasts, and mountains throughout tropical areas.

Although they cover only about 2 percent of the world's surface area, tropical rainforests are home to millions of animals (mostly insects) and plants. Scientists think that there are still many more millions of new rainforest species that have yet to be discovered.

A tropical rainforest is really four layers of plants stacked one atop another. Each layer is like a neighborhood. Each has its own animals and plants that are best suited to the amount of sunlight the neighborhood receives. From the top down, the layers of a rainforest are called the emergent layer, the canopy, the understory, and the forest floor.

The tops of the tallest trees in many rainforests form the emergent layer, often 250 feet high or more, about the height of a 25-story skyscraper. The emergent layer receives the most sunlight, heat, wind, and rain. Directly below, enormous tree leaves and branches spread out into a thick, dense layer forming the canopy. The canopy also soaks up the sun's rays, but the understory and the forest floor are dark.

Most of the plant food is located in the top layers of rainforests. This is home to "flying" squirrels; long-armed howler and spider monkeys; brilliantly colored birds; and snakes, frogs, butterflies, and uncounted millions of other kinds of insects.

In the canopy, plants such as some orchids and mosses often grow on other plants and have no roots in the ground. These "air plants," called epiphytes, absorb the minerals they need from dust in the air and rain. A bromeliad is an epiphyte in the pineapple family whose leaves funnel raindrops into a mini-pond in the middle of the plant. Wriggling insect larvae, tadpoles, tiny lizards, and crabs may live in these sky-high leaf mini-ponds.

Looping, tangled vines and lianas (woody vines) make it difficult to see the rainforest canopy from below. So scientists climb canopy sky walkways to find out what's there. The canopy is home to an amazing variety of living things: As many as fifty different kinds of orchids can grow on a single tree.

Plants grow in the dark and shadowy understory and floor. Even on a sunny day, only a small amount of light penetrates the thick green foliage above. Here, trees still grow tall quickly, vines grow to a half mile in length, and some kinds of tropical bamboo plants grow more than a foot a day.

A rainforest floor is covered with dead and decaying leaves, fallen branches, ferns and other small plants, molds and mushrooms, thick roots of giant trees, and small tree saplings. The floor swarms with different insects, worms, land snails, frogs, toads, snakes, birds, and small rodents.

Millions of army ants can be found marching in columns for hours, days, or even weeks. The huge numbers of ants produce a faint hissing sound and a sharp acid odor. Army ants can eat tens of thousands of insects each day. They can kill and eat even larger animals, including lizards, snakes, and birds, but they are not usually dangerous to people. Humans can just step aside as the ant columns pass by.

The Amazon River, the largest river in the world, has more than one thousand tributaries and a total water flow that is greater than the next eight largest rivers combined. Oceangoing ships can travel thousands of miles inland up the Amazon. This massive river flows through the largest tropical rainforest in the world.

Thousands of different kinds of fish and other animals have been found in the Amazon River. The arapaima, the largest freshwater fish in the world and a member of the catfish family, lives there. It can reach a length of close to 10 feet and can weigh more than 400 pounds.

The Amazon is also home to the anaconda, the heaviest snake in the world. The anaconda is a constrictor; the snake coils its powerful body around its victim until it suffocates. Then the anaconda unhinges its huge jaws and swallows its prey whole.

More than a thousand different kinds of frogs live in the Amazon rainforest. Each frog species makes its own special kind of croaking, whistling, grunting, or chirping sounds.

Frogs must keep their skin moist. Unlike frogs of temperate regions that live in or near ponds, tropical frogs can live anywhere in a rainforest because of the high humidity and frequent rainstorms. Rainforest frogs can live in trees and even lay their eggs on leaves.

Dart poison frogs often have brilliant colors and patterns advertising to enemies that they are poisonous. The red-eyed tree frogs of Central America hide in trees in the daytime. In Asian rainforests, the flying frog glides away from danger on "parachutes" of skin stretched between its toes.

More than five thousand species of birds live in tropical rainforests, including more than three hundred types of parrots, such as macaws, cockatoos, and parakeets. They all have bright colors, loud calls, powerful beaks, and feet with two toes facing forward and two facing backward. Parrots feed on seeds, fruits, and leaves. The Southeast Asian hanging parrot sleeps upside down by using its toes to hang from branches.

Parrots come in all sizes. The 40-inch-long hyacinthine macaw of Brazil weighs almost 4 pounds, but a pygmy parrot is as small as your finger and weighs as much as a few coins. Along the banks of the Amazon River, flocks of multicolored macaws gather by the hundreds and thousands. In Southeast Asian and Australian rainforests, you will see cockatoos instead of macaws.

Sloths are rainforest canopy mammals. Their flat faces, beady eyes, strange-looking fur, long arms, and threatening claws may make you think of aliens from a science fiction movie. The three-toed sloth eats leaves.

A tapir looks like a mixture of a pig and a small hippopotamus. Tapirs live in swampy rainforest spots. They eat leaves, fruits, and other plant foods. Tapirs live in Central and South American rainforests.

The scaly, smelly pangolin lives in African and Asian rainforests. It breaks open logs with its large, powerful claws and laps up ants with its long, slender tongue. When it is threatened, a pangolin rolls into a ball and looks like a big pinecone. The pangolin is not closely related to any other living mammal.

Bats make up the largest number of mammals in a rainforest. Bats range in size from the giant flying fox of Malaysia, with a wingspan of 5 to 6 feet, to the tiny bumblebee bat of Thailand, the smallest mammal in the world, which weighs about as much as a dime and is about 1 inch long. The giant flying fox is a fruit-eating bat. The bumblebee bat is an insect eater.

Most rainforest bats eat fruit or insects and other small animals. However, vampire bats, found only in Central and South America, come out at night to feed on the blood of cows and other mammals. They rarely bite people.

A rainforest canopy is home to many kinds of monkeys and apes. The spider monkey uses its long tail to swing back and forth like an acrobat. Howler monkeys cry loudly at daybreak and nightfall. Each rainforest has its own monkey or ape species. Some of the largest apes in the world are the gorillas and chimps that live in African rainforests and the long-armed gibbons of Southeast Asia.

Rainforest animals have special abilities and adaptations that help them survive. The yellow-banded poison frog's beautiful skin colors warn away enemies. These frogs are so poisonous that contact with their skin can kill you. In the Amazon rainforest, some hunters tip arrows or darts with frog-skin poisons.

The king cobra is a venomous snake that lives near rivers and swampy areas in Southeast Asian rainforests. It can grow from 12 to 18 feet long and its fangs are a half inch in length. When a king cobra feels threatened, it forms a hood by raising the front part of its body off the ground.

The red-bellied piranha is less than a foot long, yet it is more feared than the giant anaconda. The piranha is armed with rows of very sharp triangular teeth that can cut through almost anything, even cattle. Piranhas can strip an animal of all its flesh within a matter of minutes.

There are many hidden dangers in rainforests, including "bullet" ants, whose sting is terribly painful, as well as other insects, spiders, scorpions, small animals, and plants. Some scorpions make venom inside their bodies. This 10-inch Amazonian giant centipede has a venomous bite.

Some caterpillars can eat poisonous plants without being harmed. But as butterflies, they become poisonous. When a bird eats a poisonous butterfly, the bird becomes sick. It learns to avoid butterflies such as this postman butterfly.

Poisons that can be helpful to people include curare, a substance found in the bark and roots of certain vines. While it can paralyze an animal, it can also be used as a medicine to treat bruises and fever.

Rainforests are extremely important to the world's climate and to the health of our environment. Trees and other plants in the rainforests retain billions of tons of carbon in their trunks, stems, and leaves. If the carbon were released into the air in the form of carbon dioxide, the greenhouse effect, global warming, and climate change would be impacted in a significant way. People rely on rainforests as the source of many products, including medicines, timber, fruits such as bananas and mangos, nuts, oils, and spices. This affects the way rainforest farmers make their land-use decisions. In one way or another, people are connected to and interdependent with rainforests.

Our rainforests are in danger. Every year, more than 25,000 square miles of rainforests, an area about the size of the state of West Virginia, are cut down and the land is cleared for farming, cattle grazing, or mining. Ironically, the soil of a rainforest is poor in nutrients and not even very good for farming.

After a rainforest has been slashed and burned, it can take one hundred years or longer for it to grow back to what it was. Tropical rainforests are important to all of us around the world, not just in the countries where they are found. And there is so much yet to learn about them. But first, we all need to find ways to help tropical rainforests survive.

GLOSSARY

Biodiversity—The number and variety of plants, animals, and other living organisms found in a specific geographic region.

Canopy—The second-highest rainforest layer, formed by the leaves and branches of the tops of trees.

Climate—The weather conditions in one place over a long period of time.

Climate change—A significant change in the weather in an area over a long period of time that can be natural or caused by changes people have made to the land or atmosphere.

Emergent layer—The topmost layer of the rainforest that extends above the canopy.

Epiphyte—A plant that grows on another plant.

Equator—An imaginary circle around the earth, dividing the earth's surface into the northern and southern hemispheres.

Forest floor—The bottommost layer of the rainforest.

Global warming—A term used to describe increases in the earth's average temperature.

Greenhouse effect—A process by which the buildup of certain gases prevents the heat that enters the earth's lower atmosphere as sunlight from escaping back out into space.

Larva—A life stage of an insect as it develops from an egg into an adult. The larva of an insect looks completely different from how it will look as an adult.

Temperate region—The area of the earth between cold polar and hot tropical regions.

Tributary—A stream or river that flows into another, larger river.

Tropical—Describes a place near the equator where weather is hot and humid.

Understory—The layer of the rainforest just above the forest floor, made up of plants that grow in the shade.

INDEX

Bold type indicates illustrations.

Africa, 6
Amazon rainforest, 14, 17, 25
Amazon River, 14, 18, **28**
Amazonian giant centipede, 26, **27**
Apes, 22
  Chimps, 22
  Gibbons, 22
  Gorillas, 22
Arapaima, 14
Army ants, **12**, 13
Asia, 6, 22

Bamboo, 13
Bats, 22
  Bumblebee, 22
  Giant flying fox, 22
  Vampire, 22, **23**
Bromeliad, 10, **11**
Butterflies, 9, 26
  Postman, **26**

Canopy, **8**, 9, 10, 21, 22
Carbon, 29

Carbon dioxide, 29
Caterpillars, 26
Central America, 6, 17, 21, 22
Climate change, 29
Curare, 26

Emergent layer, **8**, 9
Epiphytes, 10, **11**

Ferns, 13
Forest floor, 9, 13
Frogs, 5, 9, 13, 17, 25
  Dart poison, **11**, 17, **17**
  Flying, 17, **17**
  Red-eyed tree, **6**, **16**, 17
  Yellow-banded poison, 25

Global warming, 29
Greenhouse effect, 29

Humidity, 17

Insects, 5, 6, 9, 10, 13, 22, 26

Lianas, **2**, **4**, **6**, 10, **10**
Lizards, 10, 13

Malaysia, 22
Medicine, 26, 29
Monkeys, 9, 22
  Howler, 9, 22
  Spider, **3**, **7**, 9, 22

Orchids, 10

Pangolin, 21, **21**
Parrots, 18
  Cockatoos, 18
  Macaws, **6**, 18, **18**, **19**
  Hyacinthine, 18
  Parakeets, 18
  Pygmy, 18

Southeast Asian hanging, 18
Poison, 17, 25, 26

Rain, 5, 9, 10
Red-bellied piranha, **24**, 25

Scorpions, 26
Snails, 13
Snakes, 9, 13, 14, 25
  Anaconda, 14, **15**, 25
  King cobra, 25
South America, 6, 22

Tapir, 21, **21**
Thailand, 22
Three-toed sloth, **20**, 21

Understory, 9, 13

Venom, 26

READ MORE ABOUT IT

Smithsonian Institution
www.si.edu

Rainforest Action Network
www.ran.org

Rainforest Alliance
www.rainforest-alliance.org

GORILLAS
by Seymour Simon

SNAKES
by Seymour Simon

SPIDERS
by Seymour Simon